Candlelight Writers Inc

Copyright© 2020 by Wanda Kay Knight

Library of Congress Control Number: 2020937055

Paperback ISBN: 979-8-9881788-5-9

Illustrations: Sandamali Kamalchandra

10 9 8 7 6 5 4 3

Courageous Kids

Charles Dickens
The Blacking Factory

Written By Wanda Kay Knight

Illustrated by Sandamali Kamalchandra

Scotsland

England

Ireland

London

Wales

Portsmouth

Map of
ENGLISH
ISLES

Who: Charles Dickens
When: Born 1812
Where: Portsmouth and London, England
What: Author

Charles had a wonderful and happy family. They lived in a lovely house and they had great friends.

Charles loved to read! He read all the time.

He also wrote stories. His friends said that he wrote the best stories ever!

Charles dreamed that someday he would be a scholar and a gentleman.

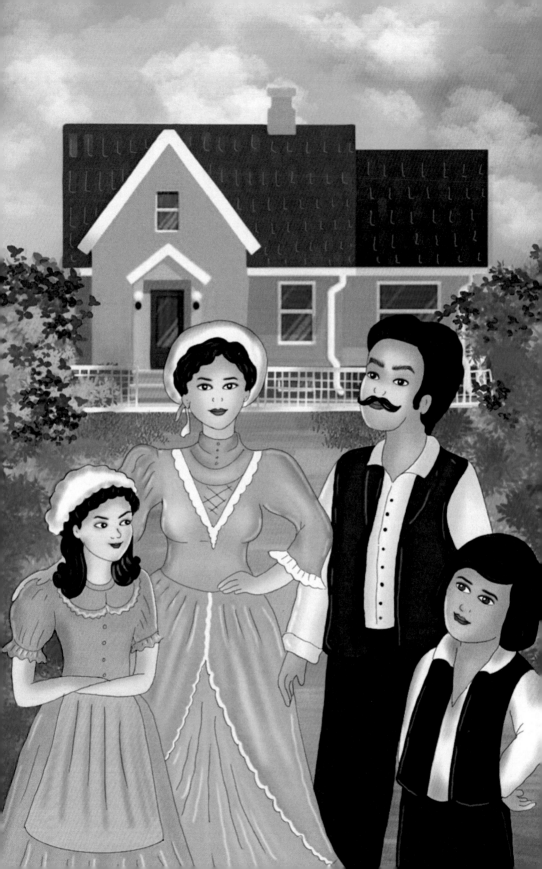

When Charles was eleven years old, his life changed very suddenly.

His parents seemed a little upset. The family packed their stuff and they all moved into a new house.

When Charles saw the new house, he was surprised. It was much smaller than his old house.

The yard was not nearly as nice.

His parents didn't seem happy very often.

Charles' father and his mother whispered and shook their heads as they wrote out figures and numbers on paper.

Sometimes, Charles could hear the floorboards squeak as his father paced the floor at night.

Charles knew something was very wrong.

When it was time for school to begin, his parents shook their heads.

"Charles," they said, "you cannot go back to school. There is only enough money to send your sister to school. You cannot go."

"What?" Charles cried. "But I love school. Please let me go!"

But he could not go to school. When he watched his older sister leave, tears rolled down his face.

While his sister was at school, Charles helped his parents. He took care of his younger siblings.

But then, things got even worse. His parents had to sell some of the furniture to make money. Before long, the house was almost empty.

Even during those hard times, Charles kept reading the books he loved. He kept hoping that things would turn around so that he could go back to school.

Every day he kept reading and hoping that his parents would send him back to school.

But instead of things getting better, they got even worse!

One day, when Charles was twelve years old, his mother said she needed to talk to him.

"Charles," she said, "you will have to go to work at the blacking factory to make money for the family. It's the only way."

Charles was shocked. He wanted to go to school. He did not want to work at the blacking factory.

The blacking factory was in an
old tumble-down building
beside the river.

It had rotten floors and a
rotten staricase. It was old
and it smelled like mold.

Rats were swarming in the
cellar of the old building. Lots
and lots of rats!

Charles walked to the factory every morning at eight o'clock.

He worked until eight o'clock every night.

He worked six days a week in a miserable, dirty room.

While he was working, he thought about his books, and his friends, and his school.

He hoped things would get better so that he would not have to work in the old, stinky factory anymore.

He wanted his family to be together again.

Charles covered shoe polish bottles with paper and labels.

Then, he tied a string around the bottles.

The bottles of shoe polish were taken to the stores so people could keep their shoes looking good.

While he worked, Charles could hear the rats squeaking and swarming in the cellar. Sometimes he saw rats.

Oh, how he hated those rats!

But then, something even
worse happened.

In those days, a person could
be sent to jail if they did not
pay their debts.

Charles' father could not pay
his debts back.

Charles' father was arrested
and taken away to prison.

The entire family, except for
Charles, went to live in the
jailhouse with the father.

Charles did not have to go to jail. But he did have to keep working.

Charles stayed by himself in a cheap boarding house.

Every day he got up and walked to work by himself.

At eight o'clock in the evening, when work was done, he walked home by himself.

He fixed his own supper to eat. Then he read for a while before he went to bed.

Charles wanted to live with his family. He wanted to go back to school. He hated the dirty rat-filled factory.

It took about a year, but finally, something really wonderful happened to Charles and his family.

Charles' father inherited money. He paid all of his debts off.

The entire family got out of jail. Then, they all moved into the boarding house with Charles.

It was so wonderful to have his family back home!

His family was home!

But, something else
wonderful happened!

Charles got to go back to
school. He had friends again!

He read books. He studied.
He wrote stories. He had fun
with his friends.

For two years, his life was
back to normal. Charles was
happy!

Sadly, after two years, it all changed again.

His father had money troubles again.

Again, Charles had to leave school and work to make money for the family.

But this time, it was different!

This time when Charles went back to work, he was fourteen years old!

Because he was fourteen, he was able to get a job as a law clerk. He really liked being a law clerk.

He also remembered his dream of being a scholar and a gentleman.

And because he remembered his dreams, he began doing want he always wanted to do.

He began writing stories!

What
Happened?

By the time he was twenty-four years old, Charles was publishing "The Pickwick Papers."

In London, crowds would stand on the street corners and listen while people read his stories. Later, he put his stories into books.

We still read his books today.

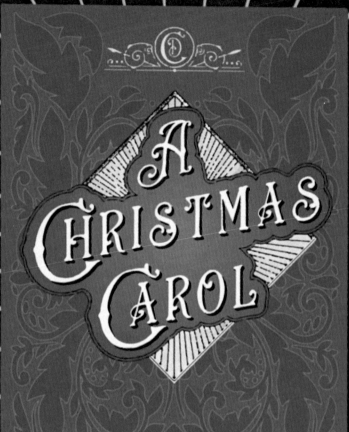

Another book that Charles wrote is named, "A Christmas Carol."

In that story, the ghosts of Christmas teach a very crabby man named Scrooge how to be a happier person.

But, Charles also wrote a lot of stories about kids who had to go to work in terrible places. Some of the children were homeless, too.

When people read the stories, they started to think about the children who had to work long hours.

Finally, people made laws so that boys and girls could not work long hours in factories. Because of the changes, boys and girls got to go to school.

Charles Dickens changed his world
by remembering his dreams,
caring about poor children, and
writing stories.